HIS

Faith

"POSITIONS US FOR POSSESSION"

APMI Publications
a division of Kingdom Dimension Books
P.O. Box 17,
55051 Barga (LU),
Tuscany, Italy

HIS *Faith*

DR. ALAN PATEMAN

BOOK TITLE:
His Faith, Positions us for Possession

This edition published in 2020

Published by APMI Publications
A Division of Kingdom Dimension Books, Library No. **13**
P.O. Box 17,
55051 Barga (LU),
Italy

Email: publications@alanpatemanworldmissions.com
www.AlanPatemanWorldMissions.com

**APMI Publications and Kingdom Dimension Books are a division of
Alan Pateman World Missions**

Printed in the United States of America, Europe and Asia

Paperback ISBN: 978-0-9570654-0-6
eBook ISBN: 978-0-9518746-2-2

Acknowledgements:
Author/Design/Senior Editor/Publisher: Apostle Dr. Alan Pateman
Editing/Proofreading/Research: Dr. Jennifer Pateman
Computer Administration/Office Manager: Dr. Dorothea Struhlik
Cover Image Credit: www.PosterMyWall.com

*Unless otherwise indicated, all scriptural quotations are from the King James Version of the Bible. Where scriptures appear with special emphasis (**in bold,** italic or <u>underlined</u>) we have edited them ourselves in order to bring focused attention within the context of this subject being taught.*

❖

Dedication

I would like to dedicate this book to A.J and Naomi who have both operated in such simple faith as we have travelled from one country to the next! Their resilience and unequalled trust in their Daddy and Mummy has been such a witness and example to all of us as we have trusted our Heavenly Father on this journey of discovery!

Jesus told us to come unto Him as children with simple faith in His ability; taking on *"His Faith,"* while He directs our steps. *"Verily I say unto you, Except ye be converted, and become as little children, ye shall not enter into the kingdom of heaven"* (Matthew 18:3).

We love you guys - you are an inspiration! You are both so highly blessed. May God continue using you as you give Him the best years of your lives, inspiring your generation and ours.

❖

Table of Contents

❖

Foreword

Centred around the faith of the Son of God, this book appeals to all generations and walks of life. Every human being alive on planet earth today needs "the faith of the Son of God" *(Galatians 2:20)*.

No other element of existence in the universe can sustain man better. In fact nothing is more substantial or provoking than "His faith in us," and nothing compels or enthuses God's pleasure more! *(Hebrews 11:6)*

Our human faith is limited and *earth-bound*, miserly in comparison! In today's world man depends far too much on his own self-awareness. It is true that man's stubborn independence, self-reliance, even "self-worship" *(narcissism!)* and self-sufficiency have totally hindered and maligned his faith in Christ.

Today humanism prevails in our homes and in our churches; where human philosophies openly omit the *deity* of God, which is summed up precisely in 2 Timothy 3:5 as *"...having a form of godliness, but denying the power thereof."*

As a result many of our lives, churches and ministries are *dangerously impotent,* simply because we are all too reliant on *everything-other-than* God!

Even in this Hi-Tech world of ours, the truth remains the same and only as we take-on, walk-in and live-by the faith of the Son of God as Paul did, will our lives truly honour the Father and transform to resemble what God has kept in store for us *(Jeremiah 29:11; Galatians 2:20, Ephesians 3:20).*

It is with both simplicity and seasoned proficiency that Dr. Pateman draws us into this weighty conclusion;

> *...only as we yield and surrender to Christ's faith IN us – will we truly be empowered to live as Christ lived on this earth, "...as he is, so are we in this world."*
>
> *(1 John 4:17)*

❖

Introduction

Central to the theme of this book is the **"Faith OF the Son of God."** NOT the frailty of man's own faith. In order for us to live in resurrection life with Christ, we must come to this same conclusion as Paul the apostle...

I am crucified with Christ: nevertheless I live; yet not I, but Christ liveth in me: and the life which I now live in the flesh I live by the faith of the Son of God, who loved me, and gave himself for me.

(Galatians 2:20)

Many of us when first entering the Kingdom of God; having been taught that salvation was by Grace through Faith – we figured that Grace was God's part and faith was our part! His choice followed by our *(voluntary)* obligation! We fell so early on into striving to complete by the flesh what started in the Spirit; it was God's FAITH that saved us not our OWN!

> *For by grace are ye saved through faith; and that not of yourselves: it is the gift of God...*
>
> *(Ephesians 2:8)*

If "*self-effort*" can be attributed to our salvation – then let us proceed therein! But as salvation is by *GRACE* through *FAITH* let us continue likewise! "...Not by might, nor by power, but by my spirit, saith the LORD of hosts" *(Zechariah 4:6)*. We must continue as we began, by *HIS* Faith and by *HIS* Spirit of Grace *(see Zechariah 12:10; Galatians 5:16, 25)*.

There is no battle in surrender! Neither struggle nor argument with a dead man! *(Romans 6:4; 8:10-11; Ephesians 2:5)* The fight is over when we yield... "For ye are dead, and your life is hid with Christ in God" *(Colossians 3:3)*.

Evidence to distinguish whose faith we are yielding to is this; are we doing what only His Faith can do...!

> *I assure you, most solemnly I tell you, if anyone steadfastly believes in Me, he will himself be able to do the things that I do; and he will do even greater things than these...*
>
> *(John 14:12 AMP)*

When Jesus declared, "Oh ye of little faith..." *(Matthew 6:30; 8:26; 16:8; Luke 12:28)* he was stating an eternal truth, *(not just criticising His disciples!)* that our faith would NEVER be enough. The call of God is too large, the responsibilities too vast for us to approach it in our own strength or even our own faith.

Appreciably of course we can acknowledge the resourcefulness of man's natural faith; just the modern world of business with its conglomerates, skyscrapers and multi-billion dollar industries alone are witnesses enough to the fact that man's own natural faith is robust and extremely resourceful. Even New York's *altered* skyline attests man's creative ingenuity, still with its many present-day towers of Babel!

And my speech and my preaching was not with enticing words of man's wisdom, but in demonstration of the Spirit and of power: That your faith should not stand in the wisdom of men, but in the power of God.
(1 Corinthians 2:4-5)

But the Church has long enough lent itself to humanistic excuses for its lack of power. The intellect will only take us as far as our limitations! Once discovered our limitations can only humble us to acknowledge the ONE who supersedes all.

❖

CHAPTER 1

Trained Yieldedness

The Hebrew word for *"faith"* used above in Habakkuk 2:4 *'ĕmûnâh (pronounced em-oo-naw')*, #530 in *Strong's Exhaustive Concordance*, literally means *firmness; security; fidelity: - faithfulness, set office, stability, steady, truly and truth.* See also the New Testament version of the same scripture in Hebrews 10:38 *"...Now the just shall live by faith..."* However notice it omits the word *"his."*

> *Behold, his soul which is lifted up is not upright in him: but the just shall live by his faith.*
>
> *(Habakkuk 2:4)*

In the New Testament we have a greater faith to yield to than our own. This does not make our own faith obsolete, rather a "living partnership" with Christ. We are called to do a job that without God is impossible to achieve. Therefore to fulfil our New Testament Commission it takes no less than *Divine Co-operation* and *Supernatural Trust!*

At the age of 12 Jesus exhibited intelligence and dedication; not to personal ambition but to the Will of His heavenly Father; in co-operation with the Holy Spirit and with the Scriptures. If the Son of God had to *LEARN* obedience even though he was perfect, there's plenty of room for us to learn *TRAINED YIELDEDNESS.*

> *Though he were a Son, yet learned he obedience by the things which he suffered…*
>
> *(Hebrews 5:8)*

Similar to faith let us consider the fruits of the Spirit; which also require our willingness to yield. On the day of Pentecost for instance, the Holy Spirit arrived on the scene already perfect and entire, with not one seed needing to be matured or developed. *ETERNAL*; He arrived READY with a mission to endow His saints *(1 Corinthians 12:4-11; Ephesians 4:7, 11-12).*

Only as we yield to the One who is perfectly patient, loving, kind and gentle within, can we truly be recognised by our fruits! With no confusion about what spirit we are of *(Matthew 7:20; Luke 9:55).* Therefore our highest service remains to Yield.

> *Know ye not that whom ye yield yourselves servants to obey, his servants ye are to whom ye obey…*
>
> *(Romans 6:16)*

However FAITH *"IN"* THE SON OF GOD alone is clearly insufficient, even demons acknowledge Jesus having no doubt about His authority! *"*...the evil spirit answered and said, Jesus I know, and Paul I know; but who are ye?*" (Acts 19:15)* More to the point living by the FAITH *"OF"* THE SON ensures honour will go where honour is due and credit where credit is due, to God alone. No flesh can glory in His presence!

Abraham had to rely solely on his own faith; he did not have THE FAITH OF THE SON. We are part of a Better Covenant; where divine exchange occurs - all of His for all of ours. No longer do we have to solely rely on our own puny efforts. We can be trained in yieldedness and operate just like Paul the apostle - by the FAITH OF THE SON.

There was no other reason Jesus could express such confidence with this declaration; *"*...greater works than these shall ye do*" (John 14:12)* because He knew that for us to achieve *HIS MINISTRY* we would have to operate by *HIS FAITH!* "Jesus went about doing good and healing all those who were afflicted of the devil" *(Acts 10:38).*

This same ministry belongs to every believer TODAY who has the courage to yield to a *FAITH* greater than his own. We are called for such a time as this! *(Ester 4:14)* And God who freely gave us *ALL THINGS* did not neglect to give us *HIS FAITH.*

Developing a Hearing Ear

In the last 20 years of walking with the Lord I have seen much success simply by obeying HIS VOICE. This does not negate knowing His written Word of course! Nonetheless any RELATIONSHIP without *"SPOKEN"* words suffers severe limitations; even our relationship with God requires both the *logos* and *rhēma.*

Therefore even in our pursuit for knowledge we must never fail to develop a hearing ear! *"Educated Fools"* are only content to possess qualifications they will never use! But God wants us equipped with skills so that we can LIVE IN OBEDIENCE. Rightly dividing His Word with the spirit of revelation simply holds its purpose in obedience! *(2 Timothy 2:15)*

Therefore our destiny can only lie in our own hands, largely dependent on our willingness to hear God's voice and live out His instructions *(see Revelations 2:7).*

My heart aches whenever I think of so many millions living below their potential and talent levels, solely because of fear and procrastination.

> *And it shall come to pass, if thou shalt hearken diligently unto the voice of the LORD thy God, to observe and to do all his commandments which I command thee this day, that the LORD thy God will set thee on high above all nations of the earth: And all these blessings shall come on thee, and overtake thee, if thou shalt hearken unto the voice of the LORD thy God.*
>
> *(Deuteronomy 28:1-2)*

It is evident that God assigned special paths in life for all. It is our duty to find out what that path is and walk it through, with the *"Faith of the Son of God."*

For we are his workmanship, created in Christ Jesus unto good works, which God hath before ordained that we should walk in them.

(Ephesians 2:10)

Trust is at the Core

Smith Wigglesworth once said, "Only believe! God will not fail you, Beloved. It is impossible for God to fail. Believe Him. Rest in Him, for God's rest is an undisturbed place where heaven bends to meet you. God will fulfil the promises made to you in His word - believe it!"

While looking into the dynamics of faith, one could never bypass or evade the subject of *TRUST*. You simply can't have faith without trust; they are indelible and intrinsic elements of the same thing! After all who ever heard of having faith in a God who could not be trusted? Nevertheless it must be said that there are some elements of faith that go *beyond* simple trust, while trust never leaves the central core.

Foremost examples of Old Testament faith *(trust)* can be found in scriptures bearing the Hebrew words *châsâh* and *bâtach;* generally taken to mean; *have confidence in, trust, make refuge;* two examples are Psalm 36:7 and Proverbs 3:5. "How excellent is thy loving kindness, O God! therefore the children of men put their trust *[châsâh]* under the shadow of thy wings." "Trust *[bâtach]* in the Lord with all thine heart; and lean not unto thine own understanding."

To look at another example there are precious few who displayed greater trust in their God during Old Testament times, than Abraham, whose faith set things in motion that forever changed the course of human history. In fact *ALL* the *"heroes of faith"* listed in the eleventh chapter of the book of Hebrews, to whom New Testament believers look for inspiration, were *"Old Testament Individuals"* who simply put their *TRUST* in God!

Whereas *pistis (pis'-tis)* the Greek word used for *FAITH* in Hebrews 11 and Romans 10:17 – helps take things to another level! Going beyond *TRUST* to focus on getting the job done and ensuring ultimate salvation!

This little Greek word πίστις *(pistis)* is taken primarily to mean; *persuasion, moral conviction (especially reliance upon Christ for salvation); assurance, belief and fidelity.*

"Without *pistis* it is impossible to please God" *(Hebrews 11:6).* It did not say without *TRUST* it's impossible to please God. Yet faith could be called *the ultimate level of TRUST.*

Similar to *rhēma and logos – faith and trust* are akin yet have striking differences in meaning; this presents the risk that purposeful differences could be lost or kept hidden just for the sake that they walk on such similar ground.

❖

CHAPTER 2

Hope is Never Faith

In his book *"Man's Search for Meaning,"* Dr. Victor Frankl gives a moving account of how he survived the horrors of imprisonment in the Nazi concentration camps at Auschwitz and Dachau. Although Dr. Frankl did not have a Christian faith, he *held stubbornly to the hope* of victory through all the torture.

"Hope is a life resource, like food, water and air. In its absence, life ceases to have meaning and sometimes even ceases to be. Hope enables a person to rejoice in suffering and survive those zero hours, of distress and hardship. How did the three Hebrew children stand firm in their hour of conflict and crisis when they knew the drastic consequence of disobedience to Nebuchadnezzar's decree.

Today, the secret is in my heart and engulfs my whole being. As believers we stand on solid ground in these last days when God has spoken unto us by His Son 'whom he hath appointed heir of all things...' *(Hebrews 1:2a).*

Our greatest bulwark of Christian hope in any area of endeavour, including the ministry, is the absolute certainty of final victory: 'In all things we are more than conquerors through Christ.' The full realisation of this will turn you round full circle and open vistas of courage and indomitable faith through the power of the Son of God, enabling you to rise out of the quagmire to where God wants you to be."

Longsuffering Maintained by Hope

In time of trial, waiting on God means standing in earnest expectation and praying with supplications, intercessions and thanksgiving. Believers who are truly waiting on God are eagerly anticipating the manifestation of the answer to their prayers. Of course the way to develop the fruit of longsuffering is by maintaining hope:

> *For we are saved by hope (elpis): but hope that is seen is not hope: for what a man seeth, why doth he yet hope for? But if we hope for that we see not, then do we with patience wait for it.*
>
> *(Romans 8:24-25)*

This little Greek used for "hope" above is *elpis ελπις (pronounced el-pece' and taken from ε΄λπω elpo),* #G1680 in *Strong's Exhaustive Concordance* means, *to anticipate, usually with pleasure; expectation, confidence: - faith, hope.* And according to 1 Peter 1:13, of close relation; hope *elpizō* produces a longsuffering heart, "Wherefore gird up the loins of your mind, be sober, and hope to the end for the grace that is to be brought unto you at the revelation of Jesus Christ."

Hope, a Partner of Faith

Now faith is the substance (hupostasis) of things hoped for, the evidence of things not seen.

(Hebrews 11:1)

This Greek word for substance *hupostasis (pronounced hoop-os'-tas-is)* is a compound word that generally means: *setting under (support), concretely essence, or abstractly assurance - confidence, substance.* Therefore we could say that Faith helps turn *Hope* concrete!

By itself Hope doesn't arrive anywhere far! And without faith it enjoys no under-guarding or *"support."* Hope alone lacks all *"confidence;"* therefore hope and faith must remain indispensable partners.

While Hope is the visionary Faith is the substance; Faith creates *(gives substance to)* what Hope sees! Therefore our hope must be fixed on the promises of God and what He has already given us *(Hebrews 10:35; 3:6, 1 John 5:14).*

Who against hope believed in hope, that he might become the father of many nations; according to that which was spoken, so shall thy seed be. And being not weak in faith, he considered not his own body now dead, when he was about an hundred years old, neither yet the deadness of Sarah's womb.

(Romans 4:18-19)

23

Abraham fixed his hope on the promise of God; who had promised him a son. In the natural this looked impossible and *HOPELESS*. However Abraham did not view the situation through the natural; instead he viewed it through what God had *SAID* concerning it.

Only the Word of God can "paint" hope where there is no hope. If we take our eyes off of what the Word of God says, that's when we lose hope and give up. When experiencing physical distress, we will only lose hope and give up if we lose sight of *"...whose stripes ye were healed" (1 Peter 2:24).*

And we desire that every one of you do show the same diligence to the full assurance of hope unto the end: That ye be not slothful, but followers of them who through faith and patience inherit the promise.

(Hebrews 6:11-12)

During difficult and seemingly hopeless times, our top priority should be to find out what the Word of God declares to be true about our situation, *"But if we hope for that we see not, then do we with patience wait for it" (Romans 8:25).* Hope, patience, and receiving the promises all blends together beautifully; **hope produces patience, which is the preservative of faith in the fragile human heart.**

Only the child of God, who has learnt to yield his life in humble trust and obedience to his loving heavenly Father, can say during times of pleasure or times of suffering: *"My times are in thy hand..." (Psalm 31:15).* Blessed is the person who develops the fruit of longsuffering, for he will discover in his life that truly *"...all things work together for the good of them who love God, to them who are the called according to his purpose" (Romans 8:28).*

Hope a Future Success - Present Failure

Hope is a beautiful child of the senses; a word filled with fragrance but completely powerless. Most people mistake hope for Faith. But hope is always **future tense** while faith is always **present tense**. *"Now Faith..." (Hebrews 11:1).* Hope is vigorous; it is full of enthusiasm, but it never possesses anything. It is always a present failure! The very fact that one hopes for a thing proves that one does not possess it. But faith is a possessor! A taker! *(Matthew 11:12)* What a difference!

Faith is the creative element of God. Hope paints the clouds at the setting of the sun and makes the dying day look beautiful, still hope always fails! It makes the failure beautiful, yet it's nonetheless a failure! Contrariwise faith is a rugged, creative and dominating force.

Hope has no present tense blessing. The hoper lives on hopes. He admires and loves the Word, *but never ACTS upon it*. He knows it is true, and appreciates it enough to suffer for it, if necessary, but he fails in the mist of his rosy hopes! He fails because he ONLY hopes. **Whereas the BELIEVER obtains what the HOPER hopes for!**

Cast not away therefore your confidence (parrhēsia), which hath great recompense of reward.

(Hebrews 10:35)

Greek for confidence *parrhēsia* means; *all out spokenness, frankness, bluntness, assurance: - boldness of speech, confidence.*

25

We must not cast away our *"all-out-spokenness!"* nor be shy about what we hope for by faith!

Going beyond *"Hope"* and stepping into Faith no longer involves just mere admiration of the promises from afar; **Faith Positions us for Possession.** *(Faith goes after its prey under all circumstances disregarding every opposing force!)*

Usually our own physical senses oppose our faith by saying, *"It cannot be..."* where faith never ceases to declare, *"OH YES IT CAN!"* In fact it is only by faith that our hopes can be realities right *NOW!* Faith counts things *"done"* even before God has acted. This in turn compels God's action, because He is a faith God *(Romans 4:17).* We must learn to talk HIS faith talk!

The late Kenneth E. Hagin said, "I see so many Christians who are struggling to believe and struggling to have faith. Their focus is all wrong. They're focusing on their ability or inability to believe God, or 'trying' to have faith. They should simply start acting like God's Word is true. It will make all the difference in their lives! It is when we know God's Word is true and act like it's true that it becomes a reality to us. Faith is not something we have so much as it is something we do."

Our fight is a faith fight. "We wrestle not against flesh and blood, but against principalities, against powers, against the rulers of the darkness of this world, against spiritual wickedness in high places" *(Ephesians 6:12),* but we are *"More than Conquerors"* through Christ our Lord *(Romans 8:37).*

26

We have become masters of all demon forces. All sicknesses and diseases are made subject to us – to our words, when spoken in the Name of Jesus. We are their masters and we **conquer them with our** *words* – our confessions of His Word.

Not to mention Psalms 103:20 where we see angels obey the voice of His Word – whether in *OUR* mouths or His! The prerequisite is that we do indeed *GIVE VOICE* to the promises of God! *"Bless the LORD, ye his angels that excel in strength, that do his commandments, hearkening unto the voice of his word."* We have something to *"SAY!"*

Let the Redeemed of the Lord *SAY* So

Jesus cast out demons with the words of His mouth! He healed the sick with His words. He hushed the sea with His words. He caused the fig tree to wither by His words. Then He gave us the right to use His words; speaking them in His Name, with the same effect as if they had been spoken by Jesus Himself.

Thus, like Peter at the gate of the Temple, we also can say: *"In the Name of Jesus Christ, rise up."* Or like Paul when he cast the demon out of the insane woman; we too can say, *"In the Name of Jesus, I command thee to come out of her."* **According to our Expectation, Hope and Faith... there is no Limit...!**

We should treasure God's Word and exercise extreme caution with our lips as to what we say. Our confession imprisons or sets us free. We become what we say we are... After being prayed for, we no longer magnify Satan by mentioning our sickness. Instead, we confess God's Word. We confess healing instead of disease! He bore that disease. A positive confession overpowers disease, while a negative confession makes disease grow stronger. Our confession heals us or it keeps us sick.

It is not lying for us to say what God says about our bodies. So many seem to think they are telling a lie if they say, *"By His stripes I AM healed,"* while they still feel a pain. Never! This is not to say you don't still feel pain. You are ignoring the pain, not lying about it. Instead of glorifying the pain, you are confessing the Word, and glorifying the HEALER.

> *Who gives life to the dead and speaks of the nonexistent things that [He has foretold and promised] as if they [already] existed.*
> *(Romans 4:17 AMP)*

We must give God something to work with! Therefore we receive in direct proportion to our expectation. *"According to my earnest expectation and my hope"* (Philippians 1:20). Jesus expressed this same idea a couple of different ways. In Matthew 8:13 He told a Roman officer... *"As thou hast believed, so be it done unto thee..."* and in Matthew 9:29 He also said to the two blind men... *"According [in proportion] to your faith be it unto you"* (AMP). In all cases ***"expectancy"*** was the key.

Faith produces a very positive attitude, an attitude of expectancy. God has led me to realise that when I stopped confessing and thinking about and preaching the extraordinary, I had stopped expecting it. And when I let down my expectations of extraordinary events, *I wasn't giving God ANYTHING to work with.*

The Bible says, *"Faith is the substance of things hoped for"* *(Hebrews 11:1)* and *"Faith cometh by hearing, and hearing by the word of God" (Romans 10:17).* Therefore when I confess God's Word and preach it and confidently expect it to come to pass, I am giving God *"substance"* that He can use to bring the extraordinary to pass in my life.

When we get up every morning thinking and saying, *"This is the day God is going to do extraordinary things in my life,"* our expectancy goes way up! We begin to expect what we are thinking about and confessing; making provision for the extraordinary.

Remembering, "Champions never become champions, with losing information. You can't duplicate another's success, until you can duplicate another's knowledge. You will have to be connected to the same sources of information as those ahead of you, before you can reach those ahead of you. 'Uncommon Information' never comes from an 'Average Source.'" - J. Konrad Hölé

Faith develops through our *Knowledge* of God. Essentially, none of us can trust someone we do not really *know.* The more we know God and His faithfulness, His love, His character, His ways, how great He is etc., the more we can trust Him. This is the basis for true faith towards God *(compare Psalm 9:10; 1 Thessalonians 5:24).*

Know, recognize, and understand therefore that the Lord your God, He is God, the faithful God, Who keeps covenant

*and steadfast love and mercy with those who love Him and
keep His commandments, to a thousand generations…*
(Deuteronomy 7:9 AMP)

Will the *REAL* God Please Stand Up!

Continuing with this thought of *"KNOWING"* God; I
want to refer to what Pastor Dick Bernal said in his book,
"Don't Stop. Go Ahead!"

"How do we squeeze God into moulds? The Baptist or
evangelical type of God is a pretty good old boy who doesn't
require much. Just pray a sinner's prayer and once you're
saved you are always saved. Apparently, God grew a little
tired of miracles and the gifts of the Spirit because he did
away with them. He likes softball games, barbecues, and
social gatherings. He's not a bad guy!

The Roman Catholic type of God is mysterious and
remote. In fact, you have to approach Him through a priest.
He likes Byzantine and Gothic architecture, stained glass,
incense, and rituals. He's very mystical. The Presbyterian, or
denominational type of God, wears a three-piece suit, drives
a BMW, and doesn't require anything of His people.

Then we have certain sects of Pentecostals where God is
always angry. He won't let women wear makeup. He doesn't
believe in co-ed swimming. He won't let His people dance or
go to movies. He's no fun at all!

Some 'hyper-faith' circles portray God as a big computer
in the sky. You just program Him with your requests and out
comes the new car and bigger home! Or sign a pledge for ten

percent of your income so that He will automatically send you a rebate in the amount of times you're offering.

Okay, I'm stereotyping, but bear with me while I make a point. What do we tell a world that is crying out to know God? Which version of God is right? The Baptist, the Catholics, the Presbyterians, the Pentecostals, or the other offshoots that are too numerous to mention?

Actually, all of these approaches offer something of the richness of Jesus. Paul admonishes us to encourage one another, being knit together in love, that we might attain 'all riches of the full assurance of understanding, to the knowledge of the mystery of God, both of the Father and of Christ, in whom are hidden all the treasures of wisdom and knowledge' *(Colossians 2:2-3).*

But these riches can be lost when one is jockeying for supremacy. Maybe it's time to stop pointing at each other in accusation or defence, and start pointing to Christ Himself. He is asking each one of us if we love Him."

If our faith truly develops through our **Knowledge** of God, then we better know who we worship and who we trust! *"For as I passed by, and beheld your devotions, I found an altar with this inscription, TO THE UNKNOWN GOD" (Acts 17:23).*

Beloved, let us love one another, for love is (springs) from God; and he who loves [his fellowmen] is begotten (born) of God and is coming [progressively] to know and understand God [to perceive and recognize and get a

31

better and clearer knowledge of Him]. He who does not love has not become acquainted with God [does not and never did know Him], for God is love.

(1 John 4:7-8 AMP)

❖

CHAPTER 3

Grace Undeserved

Only the death and resurrection of Jesus can alter mankind's relationship with God. In His grace, God made a personal sacrifice and offered the fruits of it to us. More than simply a free gift grace is defined by this simple illustration. If I were to tap you on the shoulder today and say, *"Here are the keys to a Rolls-Royce,"* that would make a pretty large gift!

The Fruits of Grace – Yours by Faith Alone

However if your normal circumstances meant that you could obtain one by yourself if you chose to save enough or you were somehow naturally in line to inherit one anyway then the car I gave you, nonetheless a *GIFT* would still not have been a gift of grace.

Conversely if it had been totally "impossible" for you to buy a Rolls-Royce under your own means - with no natural inheritance for you to receive one - then I came along and just gave you one, only then could it be considered *"a gift of grace."* Because obviously, you couldn't possibly return the favour, in fact all you could do is say, *"Thank you,"* and accept it!

You never earn grace! If God did not give you salvation, could you obtain it any other way? No, ***Impossible!*** This is why Jesus says that He is the only way to God. There are no alternatives. If it were not by grace then maybe Krishna's idea, that there are many ways to God, could be true and several world religions would work. But there is only one way to God. His name is Jesus of Nazareth. His death and resurrection alone have made grace available to us.

He says Himself in John 14:6,

I am the way, the truth, and the life. No one comes to the Father except through Me.

This covers more than forgiveness of sins and the new birth. When you are born again as a Christian, the same applies to everything you receive by God's grace. This means that God can give you grace without you getting the praise for it and without overriding your free will. And this is only possible through faith: and that not of yourselves;

...it is a gift of God: Not of works, least anyone should boast. For we are His workmanship, created in Christ Jesus unto good works, which God hath before ordained that we should walk in them.

(Ephesians 2:8-10)

Defining Grace

But the LORD was with Joseph, and showed him mercy, and gave him favour (chên) in the sight of the keeper of the prison.

(Genesis 39:21)

The Hebrew word **chên** *(pronounced khane)*; #H2580 in *Strong's Exhaustive Concordance*; fundamentally means; *graciousness, kindness, favour, beauty, pleasant, precious.* And then in close relation the word **chânan** *(pronounced khaw-nan)* means; *to bend or stoop in kindness to an inferior; to show favour and to have mercy.*

The concept of grace is many-sided and subject to development in the Scriptures. In the Old Testament **chên,** *"Favour,"* is the unmerited favour of a superior to an inferior. In the case of God to man; **chên** is demonstrated usually in temporal, though also occasionally in spiritual blessings; within deliverance in both physical and spiritual senses *(Jeremiah 31:2; Exodus 33:19).*

Also in the Old Testament **chêsêd** *"Loving-Kindness,"* is the firm loving-kindness expressed between related people and particularly in the covenants into which God entered with His people and which His **chêsêd** firmly guaranteed *(2 Samuel 7:15; Exodus 20:6).* "But my mercy *(chêsêd)* shall not depart away from him, as I took it from Saul, whom I put away before thee" *(2 Samuel 7:15).*

Greek literature gave *charis* the following meanings:

1. *One that causes attractiveness, such as grace of appearance or speech.*

2. *Favourable regard felt toward a person.*
3. *A favour.*
4. *Gratitude.*
5. *It was used adverbially in phrases such as "for the sake of a thing," charin tinos.*

The little word χάρις **charis** *(pronounced khar'-ece), used in* John chapter one and verse seventeen, "...the law was given by Moses, but grace *(charis)* and truth came by Jesus Christ," also found in the *Strong's Exhaustive Concordance* under **#G5485** means; *graciousness, ...divine influence upon the heart, and its reflection in the life; gratitude, acceptable, benefit, favour, gift, grace, joy, liberality, pleasure, thankworthy.*

But it's important to point out that it was not until the coming of Christ that grace took on its fullest meaning. His self-sacrifice was grace itself *(2 Corinthians 8:9)* and is absolutely free *(Romans 6:14; 5:15-18; Ephesians 1:7; 2:8-9)*. When the believer receives grace, it governs his or her spiritual life by compounding favour upon favour. It equips, strengthens, and controls all phases of the believer's life *(2 Corinthians 8:6-7; Colossians 4:6; 2 Thessalonians 2:16; 2 Timothy 2:1)*. Consequently, the Christian gives thanks *(charis)* to God for the riches of grace in His unspeakable gift *(2 Corinthians 9:15)*.

Doorway to Freedom

The apostle Paul was the principal human instrument to convey the fullest meaning of grace in Christ. The New Testament offers grace to all, in contrast to the Old Testament, which generally restricted the offer of grace to God's elect people Israel. Grace in its fullest definition is

God's unmerited favour in the gift of His Son, who offers salvation to all and who gives to those who receive Him as their personal Saviour added grace for this life and hope for the future.

Sovereign grace is not an arbitrary display of God's grace. In order to receive it man must believe. In order to enjoy it the believer must be obedient. Grace provides *Acceptance (Romans 3:24)*, *Enablement (Colossians 1:29)*, *a New Position (1 Peter 2:5, 9), and an Inheritance (Ephesians 1:3, 14)*. At least three motives are indicated in the New Testament as to why God acts in grace, especially in salvation.

He does it to **Express His Love** *(Ephesians 2:4; John 3:16)*, to be able to **Display His Grace in the Ages to come** *(Ephesians 2:7)*, and that **Redeemed man will Produce Good Works** *(Ephesians 2:10)*. Sovereign grace is always purposeful, for the life under grace is a life of Good Works.

"Man now enjoys a position in Christ before God as though he had never transgressed. He has no sense of guilt, shame or lack, only an overwhelming consciousness of having 'come home,' along with gratitude and love for Jesus, who has so graciously done it all for him. Since God has accomplished this in Christ Jesus, it is a matter of grace, rather than self-effort. Man has nothing of which he can boast. Those things in which he does boast are his cardinal sins — pride, personal achievement, self-importance and rebellion toward God's ways.

Every route to self-exaltation and 'self-salvation' for man is effectively sealed! No grounds for bartering exist between him and God where God must do His part and man his. No, it is all God's work! God took the initiative, He made the plans, He initiated them and completed them. God saved man, who was deep in sin, without his suggestions, efforts or help at all. Salvation is entirely due to God's grace. No religious, idealistic, political or philosophical ideas or deeds will take you to God. No rituals, ceremonies, pilgrimages, fasts, donations or other so called good deeds or religious habits will bring you nearer to Him.

God will only accept your admission that you can do nothing, that you are spiritually bankrupt. Then, as you receive by faith, His gift, His grace and all that He has done for you in Christ Jesus, you will be saved. Your sins will be forgiven as you are cleansed in the blood of Jesus. Then the Spirit of God will come to you and you will be born again. You will become a child of God and find peace with Him. Then you will be a Christian who, by faith in Christ Jesus, is pardoned, forgiven and justified by grace." - Ulf Ekman

> ...know that a man is not justified by observing the law, but by faith in Jesus Christ. So we, too, have put our faith in Christ Jesus that we may be justified by faith in Christ and not by observing the law, because by observing the law no-one will be justified.
>
> (Galatians 2:16 NIV)

God communicates His thoughts through His Word. When He enables us to hear what He is saying to us by the Spirit, this should create within us the response of believing or being persuaded that what He is "say-i-n-g" is indeed true and for us. "Faith comes by hearing, and hearing by the (specific) word of God" (Romans 10:17 AV).

Rhēma vs. Logos

The Greek word **rhēma** *(pronounced hray'-mah)* fundamentally means; *utterance (individually, collectively or specifically); ...saying and word.* Basically; *the "Individual Sayings of God."* But before we focus on **rhēma** let's first take a look more closely at *Logos.* W.E. Vine, in his expository dictionary of New Testament words, said that *Logos* is the *"Revealed Will of God"* and is used as the *"Sum of the Utterances of God."*

However Strong's Concordance says of *Logos* that it is the *"Divine Expression of God."* So as we hold our Bibles in our hands we are literally holding the *"Sum total of the Combined sayings of God"* in our hands... the Logos of God. Reading our Bibles then is indispensable and essential for us to know the *"Revealed Will of God"* for our lives.

As we turn our attention back on **rhēma,** first let it be said that some scholars have made the words *logos* and **rhēma** very similar in meaning; nevertheless there remains a **striking difference!** However we are first attracted to **rhēma** in Luke 1:37 *"For no word (rhēma) of God shall be void of power."* This indicates that **rhēma** as opposed to *logos* is the *"Singular Saying of God,"* rather than the *"Combined Sayings of God."*

Jesus said in Matthew 4:4; *"It is written, Man shall not live by bread alone, but by every word (rhēma) that proceedeth out of the mouth of God."* Then of course Ephesians 6:17; uses **rhēma** in connection with the sword of the Spirit. But W.E. Vine states that this is not a reference to the whole Bible as such, but to **Individual Scripture; rhēma** therefore clearly is not the picture of a man throwing the *entire* Bible at the devil; rather quoting precise, appropriate scriptures; skilfully and rightly divided!

While looking at this subject one must also consider the obvious fact that while many read their Bibles they still lack in faith; evidence enough that faith doesn't come merely by *READING* one's Bible! Romans 10:17 says; *"Faith cometh by hearing, and hearing by the rhēma of God." **Therefore, FAITH comes by hearing the SPOKEN, INDIVIDUAL SAYINGS of God**; (which of course involves QUOTING the Logos!)* For a simple and humorous illustration I eagerly quote Roy Hick's account of a Wednesday night prayer meeting in a typical evangelical church...!

"We've had a good lively song service, the leader then asks for a scripture shower. First of all, usually, there is a long silence. Then some dear, little saint of God remembers that she can quote the first verse of the 23rd Psalm. She does... and we admit that it is a wonderful verse of scripture. But what happens? Silently, to themselves about half of the congregations says, 'There goes my verse.'

Next, some Sunday School child remembers that he has learned John 3:16. He quotes it, and the rest of the congregation says, 'There goes my verse.' Humorous? Yes, but it should not be so. To be so destitute of ability to speak the word, fitly, for every occasion or every trial of our faith, is to leave ourselves open to unlimited attacks of the enemy. The Christian is clothed with defensive armour. The only offensive weapon the Christian has is the sword of the Spirit, which is the Word of God *(rhēma).* Faith cometh by hearing the Word *(rhēma)."*

Having faith involves relying on *"Revelation Knowledge"* opposed to *"Sense Knowledge,"* as best described in Hebrews 11:1 by the Amplified Bible; *"[faith perceiving as real fact what is not revealed to the senses]." "Sense Knowledge"* is knowledge that comes to the natural man through his five senses. This is limited knowledge and is described as the wisdom of man *(1 Corinthians 2:4-6).*

Revelation knowledge is knowledge, not based on the five senses or natural reasoning, but upon a higher source, the truth of the Word of God. It is revealed by the Holy Spirit to the spirit of man and it is described as the wisdom of God *(1 Corinthians 2:7-16).*

"Revelation Knowledge" is what we need, not only for ourselves but also for the spiritual atmosphere *(Ephesians 3:10)* plus the opponents of our faith cannot resist *"Revelation Knowledge" (Acts 6:10).* Although verse 6 of Hebrews chapter 11 says, *"…he is a rewarder of them that diligently seek him,"* our diligent pursuit is not because God is hidden or because He promises us more faith. *No! Rather we lose our Doubt, Fear and Unbelief!*

❖

CHAPTER 4

Opponents of Faith

On page 54 of his book *"Ruling over Life's Problems"* Ray McCauley wrote;

"The word 'disappointment' means to fail to satisfy an expectation. Disappointment will always be on this earth. It is not what happens. It is how we react to what happens. Disappointment can, if allowed to affect you, destroy your faith. I have seen people get so turned on to the Word of God and then get into a business deal, or believe for something and when things don't come right in the first week, they get disappointed and their faith disappears. I have seen people float on a cloud for a couple of weeks and suddenly, when things don't work out exactly as they want them, they get disappointed.

It can also cause people to backslide. I have seen more people backslide through disappointment than anything else. Disappointment in preachers. People say, 'Well, if that man is supposed to be a preacher then I think this whole thing is rubbish' and I have seen people so disappointed in other Christians that they turn their back on the Lord Jesus Christ. Even if every preacher went out and got drunk, the Word of God does not change and nor should you. Our faith is in the rock, and the rock does not change. Unfounded or imagined disappointment is common, especially in the Body of Christ."

Double Mindedness

Double mindedness stops us receiving from God, whereas doubt means: to waver in judgement, to hesitate in indecision. Most Christians are not walking in unbelief but double mindedness *(doubt)*. They believe what the Word says about a situation but have always have a *"Plan B"* if it doesn't work out! That's like going forwards only to go backwards! James 1:5-8 says; *"...let him ask in faith, nothing wavering. For he that wavereth is like a wave of the sea driven with the wind and tossed. For let not that man think that he shall receive anything of the Lord. A double minded man is unstable in all his ways."*

Unbelief is different in that it is totally **Negative, Unreasonable and not believing at all.** Whereas a doubter will contemplate, *"I believe God's Word; it's just not working for me!"* **DOUBLE MINDEDNESS!** Hebrews 3:12 says; *"Take heed, brethren, lest there be in any of you an evil heart of unbelief, in departing from the living God."* Unbelief has no intention or agenda to flow with God at all. In fact it is not double minded in its flat refusal to believe! It is hostile to God; as Hebrews clearly states, it is nothing short of *EVIL...*

Unbelief is a Satanic Force

Francis Frangipane says, "Someone will say, 'I believe that speaking in tongues is of the devil.' That is refusing God's Word not doubting it. There are many people in unbelief because they do not believe the Word of God. We have theologians saying that angels do not exist but Jesus Himself told us how the angels came and fed Him and ministered to Him and Psalm 91 speaks of angels. It is in God's Word."

There are those who say there is no devil; Jesus must have hallucinated or imagined some fascinating things in the wilderness! However the Word clearly says that the devil tempted Jesus in the wilderness and Jesus told us that we would cast out devils in His name. Sadly it is *"believers"* who suffer such unbelief! Paradoxically we have churches full of *UNBELIEVING BELIEVERS?!* What a pitiful oxymoron!

Another stronghold that oppresses man is fear, where people withdraw into their inner *"think-tanks"* in other words, internal houses-of-thought which trap them *"under house arrest!"* Outwardly they become more and more inoperative as the *paralysis* of fear slowly takes over; yet their inner world of frantic, tormenting thoughts is a world without end.

Fear is bondage, a demonic fortress. Something as seemingly trivial as "ridicule" can cause a person to "recoil" to the point of becoming completely introverted; where they inwardly refuse ever to be made "vulnerable" again. Details of the trauma may have been lost on memory but the recoiling involuntarily continues; flinching and raw-nerve-reactions become part of a person's personality; sadly bent on self-preservation.

FORGIVENESS alone releases us from those who hurt us. To the degree we forgive is the degree God restores our soul's healthy equilibrium and attitudes toward people. ***Everlasting Freedom from Fear's Cruel Bondage begins with LOVE.***

The Greek word *phobos (fob'-os)* used in 1 John 4:18 means primarily *(to be put in fear); alarm or fright; exceeding fear or terror.* Thankfully God provided the ultimate antidote, *"There is no fear (phobos) in love,"* therefore we can never fail to be confident that the same *agapē LOVE, (pronounced ag-ah'-pay)* which was shed abroad in our hearts by the Holy Spirit *(Romans 5:5)* is more than able to *"turn fear out of doors and expels every trace of terror!" (AMP).*

The stronghold of fear will be replaced by the *STRONGHOLD OF LOVE.* Victory begins with the name of Jesus in our mouths and the nature of Jesus is in our hearts. A *"house...swept and put in order"* is not merely enough *(Matthew 12:43)*; our thought-life must be occupied by the Person of Jesus Christ; who removes every negative influence as we continue our pursuit of Him.

> *(For the weapons of our warfare are not carnal, but mighty through God to the pulling down of strongholds;) Casting down imaginations, and every high thing that exalteth itself against the knowledge of God, and bringing into captivity every thought to the obedience of Christ.*
> *(2 Corinthians 10:4-5)*

"Pulling down" in the Greek *(kathairesis)* basically means, to demolish, make extinct and to destroy! Of which we must be diligent!

The Mind

You will remember that the location where Jesus was crucified was called *"Golgotha,"* which meant *"place of the skull."* If we will be effective in spiritual warfare, the first field of conflict where we must learn warfare is the battleground of the mind; i.e., the *"Place of the Skull."* For the territory of the un-crucified thought-life is the beachhead of satanic assault in our lives. **To Defeat the devil, we must be CRUCIFIED in the Place of the Skull!** We must be renewed in the spirit of our minds! True biblical obedience lies in doing the will of the Father. Seen again here in:

> *I can of Myself do nothing. As I hear, I judge; and my judgement is righteous, because I do not seek My own will but the will of the Father who sent Me.*
>
> *(John 5:30 NKJV)*

> *Most assuredly, I say to you, the Son can do nothing of Himself, but what He sees the Father do; for whatever He does, the Son also does in like manner.*
>
> *(John 5:19 NKJV)*

> *For I have not spoken of My own authority; but the Father who sent Me gave me a command, what I should say and what I should speak. And I know that His command is everlasting life. Therefore, whatever I speak, just as the Father has told Me, so I speak.*
>
> *(John 12:49-50 NKJV)*

God speaks to our spirits and then that information is delivered to the minds; Satan however has to communicate externally to our minds. Nevertheless it is the human *"mind"* where the battle is fought. Whoever gains control of the mind, gains control of the will, has the use of the body and voice, to manifest ambition or obedience *(see Isaiah 14:12)*.

We are Satan's only form of expression, so what we allow in our minds is crucial. In Luke 4:1-13 we find the devil trying to tempt and deceive Jesus in the area of His mind, his goal was to cause Jesus' disobedience and ambition. The Word of God has so much emphasis upon renewing our minds that Satan knows full-well what obedience to this principle will entail for him – *defeat!*

> *Set your minds on things above, not on earthly things. For you died, and your life is now hidden with Christ in God. When Christ, who is your life, appears, then you also will appear with him in glory. Put to death, therefore, whatever belongs to your earthly nature: sexual immorality, impurity, lust, evil desires and greed, which is idolatry. Because of these, the wrath of God is coming.*
> *(Colossians 3:2-6 NIV)*

Subliminal Advertising

We live in a world where there is a war going on to *CONTROL OUR MINDS*. And while scripture commands us to be transformed by the renewing of our minds, daily we are bombarded with debris from every direction; cunning and crafty, designed to take our focus and our vision.

So while very much contended, this subject remains in many people's eyes *(whether scientifically proven or not)* – a public phenomena. One method of subliminal influencing is that of hypnosis; which many are turning to for aid with giving up habits such as smoking; voluntarily having their mind temporarily programmed against the habit. It is believed that one can appeal to the subconscious mind with subliminal messages, sounds or pictures in order to influence an individual's behaviour.

In this brief mention of such a vast subject, one can clearly point out *(while others fiercely defend science and work hard to disclaim)* its powers of influence. Yet the same people attempting to disprove any claims of the effectiveness of subliminal advertising *(to protect their own interests of course!)* totally contradict themselves with the billions of dollars annually spent on airtime and advertising campaigns solely to *"influence people's minds!"*

And with the advent of the internet and the global village of users who daily surf the net – images and messages move more swiftly than ever before. From propaganda to pornography! However *"Subliminal Advertising"* is widely believed to have been first coined by *"James Vicary"* a market researcher, who claimed in 1957 that quickly flashing messages on a movie screen had influenced people to purchase more food and drink.

In a six-week test he flashed the slogans *"Drink Coca-Cola"* and *"Eat popcorn"* during a movie for 1/3000 of a second at five-second intervals. Vicary claimed that during the test, sales of Popcorn and Coke in the New Jersey Theater where the test was conducted increased 57.5 percent and 18.1 percent respectively.

As a result the practice of subliminal advertising was subsequently banned in the UK and Australia but not formally in the USA. Many believe that Vicary's discoveries were nothing more than a hoax, while the power of advertising undeniably lives on! Therefore an important question about subliminal perception must be: *"If it is effective how much so?"*

With two schools of thought one can argue that only minimal unconscious signals are perceived. Or that unconscious cognition is comprehensive and that much more is perceived than can be verbalised. Other attempts to influence or persuade are that of autosuggestion or the already mentioned hypnosis; where subjects are best influenced when *"RELAXED!"*

Or as *"Gary Greenwald"* preaches about other forms of influence such as *backmasking (aka backward-masking)*, these are messages that can be heard subliminally and can induce listeners towards *(in the case of rock music)* sex and drug use. Whether generally accepted as fact or not – the lifestyles of those involved is irrefutable. One would have to be blind or deaf not to see or hear the visual and verbal connections!

Entertainment aside, now for Politics! According to the Wikipedia Encyclopedia:

"Before the re-election of French president François Mitterrand in 1988, a subliminal picture of him was mixed in the title sequence of French national television daily news show, and it appeared for several consecutive days. Then during the 2000 U.S. presidential campaign, a television ad campaigning for Republican candidate George W. Bush showed words *(and parts thereof)* scaling from the foreground to the background on a television screen. When the word BUREAUCRATS flashed on the screen, one frame showed only the last part, RATS. Democrats promptly asked the FCC to look into the matter, but no penalties were ever assessed in the case." - www.wikipedia.org

So if they *REALLY* want us to believe their disclaimers that "subliminal-advertising" doesn't work, at subtly seducing or influencing our minds then honestly... Why, oh why do they insist on pouring all their money into an industry *(advertising)* that doesn't work? *What a dreadfully poor investment!*

❖

CHAPTER 5

Kingdom Faith

So in keeping with this emphasis on the Kingdom, let's move on to talk more about what the Kingdom really is all about. To begin with, when the Bible refers to the "Kingdom of God," it is actually referring to the "reign" *(authority)* of God more than the "realm" over which He rules or over which His authority resides.

In other words, it is more about His authority than anything else! However in our modern day vernacular this has gotten a little lost, either in translation or in cultural references and we tend to assume that "kingdom" refers to a "place" or "territory" more than to "authority."

Clearly this makes it vital for us to correct our focus a little so that the true context is not lost and where we can properly adhere to the true meaning of "kingdom" as seen in scripture. That kingdom is essentially more to do with reigning, ruling and exercising authority than it is about the realm where that authority functions.

I would say this is a far more dynamic concept. Much less passive! And it is within the New Testament that the predominant meaning of "Kingdom" was God's reign or rule; with any other meaning seldom used.

The Good News and Religion

For instance if we were to say, "The Gospel of the Kingdom of God," this would best be understood as *"THE GOOD NEWS OF THE REIGN OF GOD."* The Gospel is the good news and the Kingdom is his reign. Hence the good news of His reign! We must consider this and make it personal; His Kingdom is His rule, His authority and His government, therefore when we receive the Kingdom of God we automatically accept His government and rule over our lives and hearts.

To solidify this concept, we can remember what Jesus said; that we must *"receive the kingdom of God like little children" (Mark 10:15).* In other words, **we must receive the government of God over our lives in childlike trust,** because He has our best interests at heart. **Besides when He "governs" our lives, nothing else can!**

Consider this a little further. Every time we have prayed the "Lord's Prayer," we have actually petitioned God to "reign" over us, *("...thy kingdom come..." Matthew 6:10)* The correct context here is that God's "will" must be obeyed on earth just as it is in heaven! When men obey His will on earth, it is achieved in this present life; then the Kingdom of God has already come! It is already here! It is upon us! And obedience is always the key to truly dwelling in the Kingdom of God.

If we truly live in the Kingdom of God NOW, by allowing Him to govern over us, this in turn must mean that we see the things of His Kingdom coming to pass, not occasionally but regularly and routinely. We know that what is "normal" to the Kingdom of God; is not normal to this world *(healings and miracles)* but must be "common-place" to us!

When the Bible was written, the hearers of the Gospel possessed this early understanding of *"kingdom,"* and had a better grasp of its meaning than we do today. When they heard that the Kingdom of God was at hand, they understood that it meant **God's authority was being restored to the earth and that to enter the Kingdom of Heaven meant entering God's reign and experiencing the benefits of this in our immediate lives.**

Or perhaps today we would say in "real-time" which simply means "right-now!" Religion always keeps God "out-there" somewhere, but He and the rule of His Kingdom is "right-here" and "right-now!"

Many preachers have told us that entering the "Kingdom of Heaven" means going to heaven when we die. While this is true, it leaves us with very little understanding of the purposes of God and His intentions for His Church. **Failure** to preach and understand the "Kingdom" of God is the reason that few Christians live the life of "OVERCOMERS" today.

A Present Reality

It is when the Kingdom of God becomes a "present reality" and not just a "future hope," that mankind is able to enjoy the blessings of God's rule and reign in their individual lives. Where they enter the more "abundant" and "victorious" life that is promised in Scripture, yet sadly is only enjoyed by a minority of Christians today. Those who enjoy true Kingdom benefits today are not some elite group who live opulent life styles, but rather those who have genuine "...*righteousness and peace and joy in the Holy Spirit,*" as mentioned in Romans 14:17. This IS the Kingdom of God!

This is not to say that there is no future realm when Christ returns, but it opens to us the marvellous possibility that He will return to a world where His reign is already well established. Not to the fractured and feeble Church we have become, that is divided and has lost its grasp on what the true biblical concept of the Kingdom really is.

To the Church and by the Church

When the Kingdom of God is proclaimed to the Church and by the Church, we will have returned to the original biblical truth of the matter. Even more importantly, we will be obeying the instruction of our King Jesus, **to proclaim the Gospel of the Kingdom of God, hastening the day of His return.**

The Kingdom of God is the only thing that Jesus ever called the "Gospel." Few people understand this fact. And the fact remains that if we fail to proclaim the "Gospel of the Kingdom," we are not actually obeying His instruction to preach the "Good News of God's Reign and Authority!"

The government of God is the best news that anyone can ever hear, because it is God's only solution to all of man's ills. When we accept this "King Jesus" as the ultimate "ruler" of *every* aspect of our lives, then and only then can we truly experience Kingdom living as it should be, which is a righteous, peaceful and joyful life style in the presence of the Holy Spirit *(Romans 14:17)*.

As ambassadors of His Kingdom our role on this earth is to administer His Kingdom justice here - His rule, reign and righteousness. This is the role of every single believer, to reign spiritually and administer His spiritual justice in order to put into effect His Kingdom right here and right now.

To administer in the dictionary means to manage the affairs of, formerly give out, and to apply. This explains our role quite well in contemporary terms, because we have to minister into our everyday circumstances simply by applying God's spiritual truth and spiritual laws.

We do this without denying or breaching natural laws, in order to do things from a Kingdom perspective! BUT **the laws of God's Kingdom obviously supersede all others and we can apply these truths into the spiritual realm and let it take effect there.** Remember that everything originates in the spiritual realm first anyway *(Genesis 1:1-2)* and has its eventual effect here on the earth.

Take for instance such scriptures as Matthew 6:10 for example, where it says, "...as it is in heaven" and in Matthew 18:18 especially in the Amplified version where it talks about binding and losing on earth, just as it already is in heaven. **We are enforcers who enforce the things of God** but in the spirit realm FIRST. Because **that's where the struggle is, it is a spiritual battle and not one of flesh and blood** *(Ephesians 6:12).*

There are places of course where preaching is illegal and believers are forced underground but traditionally this has not hindered the gospel, on the contrary that's often when it runs the fastest, spreads hardest and supersedes all obstacles. But this is another discussion altogether!

Righteousness in an Unrighteous World

What we are talking about here is applying God's spiritual truth into the atmosphere, letting it supersedes all else; yet without breaching natural or political laws, to the best of our ability! Remember just being righteous in an unrighteous world is spiritual warfare in itself. We don't have to open our mouths and we create conflict just being here – spiritually speaking!

Even our worship is warfare, because it creates an atmosphere that is "contrary" to the atmosphere of this world. Therefore even before we open our mouths, we are not welcome! Anything we engage in is spiritual warfare! Our very presence on earth creates a contradiction and a conflict. *(Essentially we represent a real and present "resistance" to evil – particularly when yielded to the Holy Spirit.)*

Kingdom Faith... means; that everyone has the same amount of faith for *"life,"* but not the same amount of faith for *"ministry."* God has dealt to every man the *measure* of faith, that's in context with their individual ministry or call, as can be seen in Romans 12:3; *"For by the grace given me I say to every one of you: Do not think of yourself more highly than you ought, but rather think of yourself with sober judgement, in accordance with the measure of faith God has given you" (NIV).*

We have the faith to fulfil our own ministry not someone else's. Every person has their own ministry; although they vary in their growth, development, manifestation or expression it is nonetheless the same Spirit. But we still require *HIS FAITH* to succeed.

Complete Seven-Fold Salvation

Jesus paid the entire bill, to remove ALL curses from our lives. When He died, rose, and ascended, He entered heaven as our representative; poured out *HIS BLOOD* upon the mercy seat and purchased total salvation for all who would willingly receive His gift.

This total salvation can be called a *Seven-Fold Salvation,* because there are seven major areas of life where Jesus' awesome triumph *(Colossians 2:13-15)* made us Champions, to rule and reign in this life and beyond. The first area of course is *"Spiritually;"* we were reunited into right relationship *(righteousness)* with our Father for eternity. Hallelujah!

Fortunately for us we do not need to wait until Heaven to enjoy the benefits of our salvation. "I am come that they might have life, and that they might have it more abundantly" *(John 10:10)*. Jesus called us to an abundant life here and *NOW!* As Champions we must continue in following His Principles to walk abundantly in all areas of our lives:

> **Spiritually** – *Jesus purchased our reconciliation. Intimacy with the Father, Eternal life plus the Power to take this Gospel to the ends of the Earth.*
>
> **Emotionally** – *Joy.*
>
> **Family** – *Harmonious Living.*
>
> **Financially** – *Total Provision & Prosperity.*
>
> **Mentally** – *Peace from the Prince of Peace.*
>
> **Physically** – *Divine Health and Healing.*
>
> **Socially** – *Right Relationships.*

Valuable is the purchase that cost Him *EVERYTHING!* Victory in our lives is all-important to God because Jesus, our Champion, paid the ultimate price for us to walk in freedom in every area of our lives. In fact the only reason we can be confident of having sufficient faith for any task is that we live by the *FAITH OF THE SON OF GOD.* "I live," Paul said in Galatians 2:20, *"by the faith of the son of God."* Faith in God - is faith in His Word.

We must believe that we have *sufficient* faith because we have received the faith of the Son of God; we must be confident that we are *"living"* by HIS faith and not just our own.

60

Our Life Long Profession

Romans 1:17 tells us that, *"The just shall live by faith."* Faith is our lively hood. It is the source of finances, health and peace. Faith is our Profession and life focus… Kenneth Copeland says; *"We need to be professional believers! And so devoted to God that everything we do is related to Him."*

Our daily walk in His Word and His Spirit should be what we think about and talk about all the time. What's more, we must see *faith* as the *source of our income,* just as any professional looks at his or her profession.

❖

CHAPTER 6

Destiny is in our Mouth

This is not theory. It is fact. Charles Capps says, *"It is spiritual law"* and *"it works every time it is applied correctly."* **IT IS A SPIRITUAL LAW THAT GOD NEVER DOES ANYTHING WITHOUT S-A-Y-I-N-G IT FIRST.** He is a faith God who releases His faith through His Words. *"And Jesus answering saith unto them, Have faith in God" (Mark 11:22).* A more literal translation of the above verse says, *"Have the God kind of faith"* or *"the faith of God."*

Ephesians 5:1 literally tells us to be imitators of God as children imitate their parents. To imitate God, you must *talk* like Him and *act* like Him. He would not ask you to do something you are not capable of doing. Jesus Himself operated in the faith principles of Mark 11:23, and Matthew 17:20 while He was on earth. He spoke to the wind and sea.

He spoke to demons. He spoke to the fig tree. He even spoke to dead men! They obeyed His *SPOKEN WORDS...* that had power and influence.

He operated in the God kind of faith; God is a faith God. Most importantly, God released *HIS* faith through words, so we must follow suit. ***Our words are usually loaded with fear or faith, life or death*** *(see Genesis 1:3)*.

Jesus was imitating His Father and getting the same results! In John 14:12 Jesus said, *"He that believeth on me, the works that I do shall he do also; and greater..."* These principles of faith are based on spiritual laws that work for whosoever applies them and sets them in motion.

Do we really want all the negative things we have been confessing to come to pass? Do we really believe for those things to happen? Of course not! But if Jesus came to us personally and said, *"From this day forward it will come to pass, that everything that you say will happen exactly as you say it;"* it would change our vocabulary forever!

Spoken Words

Spoken words program our spirit *(heart)* either towards success or defeat. ***Words are truly containers; carrying and producing whatever they contain;*** *"...faith cometh by hearing and hearing by the Word of God"* (Romans 10:17). Faith comes more quickly when we hear ourselves quoting, speaking, and saying the same things God says. We will more readily receive God's Word into our spirits by ***hearing ourselves speaking it...*** than if we hear someone else speaking it.

64

Much of what the Father supplies to the body of Christ is furnished through our confession. This is not simply our positive, premeditated confession expressed in prayer; it consists of **everything** that comes out of our mouths. *"But I tell you, on the day of judgment men will have to give account for every idle (inoperative, nonworking) word they speak" (Matthew 12:36 AMP).*

The *International Standard Bible Encyclopedia (ISBE)* states that the Greek word *(argós)* generally used for *"idle or idleness"* in the New Testament literally meant, *inactive, useless, empty gossip, nonsensical talk.* Whereas the *Strong's Concordance #692* takes *argos (pronounced ar-gos')* as generally meaning; *inactive, unemployed; lazy, useless; barren, idle or slow.*

Our words are the overflow of and the revelation our truest heart condition! Christ, as the *"High Priest of our confession" (Hebrews 3:1)*, takes our words, whether in faith or unbelief, and allocates back to us eternal life in proportion to our words. When our tongue is unbridled, James tells us that our negative confession *"...sets on fire the course of our life, and is set on fire by hell" (James 3:6).*

In Hebrews 3:1 we are instructed to *"...consider the Apostle and High Priest of our profession, Christ Jesus."* The word translated as *profession* in that verse can also be translated as *confession.* God appointed and anointed Jesus to be *High Priest* over our confessions or our words of faith.

He is Responsible for bringing our Words to Pass

1 Corinthians 1:4-5 also tells us that Jesus enriches our utterance. That is, He takes our words of faith and enriches

them with His Anointing. So no matter how we look at it, the words we speak carry the very creative force of Almighty God behind them. They *WILL* come to pass!

God created us to be the **Prophets of our own lives!** Our destinies are within our reach – within our very mouths! It's our words - *not anyone else's* - that determine our success or failure in life *(Romans 10:8-9)*. Our words either bring good things into our lives or they bring evil things *(Matthew 12:34-37)*. Throughout the New Testament we find teaching on four basic kinds of confession:

The First Confession

Found in the New Testament is the confession of sin taught by John the Baptist and Jesus to the Jewish people in their day. This act of confession however, is not what we know today as Christian repentance. Actually, the confession of sin and water baptism that we read about in Matthew 3 and Luke 3 was also an act by the people of Israel under the Abrahamic *(or Old)* Covenant.

Prior to Jesus going to the cross, the Jews knew what it was to confess their sins and repent, but their sins were only *"covered"* in atonement by the blood of an animal, which was sacrificed once a year. It wasn't until the sacrifice of Jesus' blood that sin could actually be wiped out and not just covered up *(see Hebrews 10)*.

The Second Confession

Is described in the New Testament and applies to everyone, the confession of a sinner. It's what we now know as the prayer of salvation. In John 16, when Jesus told His disciples about the soon coming Holy Spirit, He explained that the Spirit would come to convict *"the world"* of sin. But what were these *"sinners"* to do, once convicted by the Spirit? Basically, the confession of a sinner under the New Covenant is simply, *"JESUS IS LORD."*

> *The word is nigh thee, even in thy mouth, and in thy heart: that is, the word of faith, which we preach; that if thou shalt confess with thy mouth the Lord Jesus, and shalt believe in thine heart that God hath raised Him from the dead, thou shalt be saved.*
>
> *(Romans 10:8-9)*

The Third Confession

Today, the Church is full of Christians who have no idea how to confess their sins once they do step out of fellowship with the Father - which is our third New Testament confession. The Bible says if you have sin in your life, get it out - confess it, repent of it, get rid of it. Once you do, stand on 1 John 1:9, which says, *"If we confess our sins, he is faithful and just to forgive us our sins, and to cleanse us from all unrighteousness."*

According to 1 John 1 and 2 when we are out of fellowship with the Father, when we sin - we know it. That's the time to get rid of it. ***Immediately!*** After all, 1 John 2:1 assures us that, *"If any man sin, we have an advocate with the Father, Jesus Christ the righteous."* Don't run from Him when you sin, *Run to Him.*

The moment we confessed our sin is the moment we got rid of it. By faith, we spewed it out of our mouths and God was faithful and just to forgive us and cleanse us.

The Fourth Confession

Found in the New Testament is the confession of our faith in God's Word, our faith in Christ - or His Anointing - our faith in God the Father, and our faith in the faithfulness of Jesus as our High Priest.

We must remember whatever we receive from God, we receive it by *CONFESSION*. **Our mouths are our own *"Master Key to Life!"*** Again the apostle Paul wrote to the Hebrews: *"...consider the Apostle and High Priest of our confession Christ Jesus" (Hebrews 3:1).*

To take a closer look, the word *"confession"* in the Greek actually means, *"Saying the same thing as; saying what God says."* It's an affirmation of a Bible truth we are particularly embracing, *(or)* repeating with our lips, the thing God has said in His Word, which we believe with our heart. You might say if you are mindful of the natural, you will live in the world but if you are mindful of the Lord, you will live by Faith.

What you Feed you Bread

From the Fruit of his lips a man enjoys good things, but the unfaithful have a craving for violence. He who guards his lips guards his life, but he who speaks rashly will come to ruin.

(Proverbs 13:2-3 NIV)

Our confessions - the words we constantly speak day after day - determine what we receive from God, whether it's salvation, physical healing, peace or financial prosperity. What's more, for the rest of our eternal existence, this principle of faith working hand in hand with our confession will never change. Jesus told His disciples in Mark 11:22; *"Have faith in God,"* or, as one translation puts it, *"Have the faith of God."* In verse 23, He went on to explain how that faith process works:

> *Whosoever shall say unto this mountain, Be thou removed, and be thou cast into the sea; and shall not doubt in his heart, but shall believe that those things which he saith shall come to pass; he shall have whatsoever he saith.*
>
> *(Mark 11:23)*

Faith operates by believing and saying and saying and saying. It is our confession or words of faith that bring possession. We see this in Romans 10:10 *"With the heart man believeth...and with the mouth confession is made..."* And in Matthew 12:34-35, *"Out of the abundance of the heart the mouth speaketh..."*

We lay hold of the Word by receiving it by faith and then **CONFESSING** it. This is the same process, which got us saved and the very process by which we still receive all-else that God promised. Remember, once we lay hold of the promises of God with our faith and our confession, that's when Jesus' enriching Anointing and ministry come into play.

That's why the apostle Paul told Timothy that, *"words of faith"* nourish, but idle words starve the spirit and make it weak *(1 Timothy 4:6-7)*. So let's do what Hebrews 10:23 says - Let's, *"Hold fast the profession of our faith..."* It is our **CONFESSION** of faith after all, that makes the difference to life or death.

Three Steps to Take;

1) Ask According to His Word.

2) Act on Your Faith in His Word.

3) Praise Him in Response to His Word.

❖

CHAPTER 7

In God's Ability

Faith thinks and plans in God's ability. This is especially essential for those looking to build something with and for God; there's no other way to think!

Now if Jesus is the author and finisher of our faith, anything that He is capable of starting, He is certainly big enough to finish! We must not enter into gimmicks attempting to get God's will done by method instead of by faith and by God's Word. God wants the church back in a place, where they *LIVE BY FAITH.*

In Habakkuk 2:4; it says the just shall live by His faith including three alternative references in the New Testament of the same, found in Romans 1:17; Galatians 3:11 & Hebrews 10:38. The Just shall live... by faith.

"If we live in the Spirit..." Paul says in Galatians 5:25, *"let us also walk in the Spirit."* How does one walk in the Spirit? *By...Faith!* Walking in the Spirit is also... walking *by...Faith!* *"We walk by faith and NOT by sight..."* *(2 Corinthians 5:7)*

We can walk a long way by faith, whereas sight and natural senses are limited. However we can go all the way in God because **when faith moves out, God moves in!**

Faith Fact & Feeling

In this illustration Paul Little describes another avenue of evidence for "living-faith" from his book *"Faith is for People,"*

"You may have heard the old proverb of Mr. Fact, Mr. Faith and Mr. Feeling. Mr. Fact, Mr. Faith and Mr. Feeling were walking along a very narrow wall. As long as Mr. Faith kept his eye on Mr. Fact, Mr. Feeling followed right along and they made beautiful progress. But every time Mr. Faith turned around and looked at Mr. Feeling, they almost fell off, because they were so paralysed with fear.

They just crept along inch by inch out of mortal fear. The moral of the story is that our feelings will follow our faith in the facts. Our certainty of salvation rests in the fact of what God has done for us in Jesus Christ and the fact of our personal commitment to Jesus Christ. If our faith lies in these facts, we find our feelings following along without difficulty."

This illustration makes simple some hard truths, as does the story of Bartimaeus. What an experience for him. What an experience to open one's eyes and look straight into the strong, yet tender face of Jesus! Then he saw the sunlight, the mountains of Moab, the palm trees and the walls of Jericho; then people and faces. He began to shout and jump up and down, and say, *"I can see! I can see!"*

We read in Mark 10:52 that after meeting Jesus, Bartimaeus *"followed Jesus in the way."* You receive Him today, and then you follow Him for a lifetime through a daily work of consistent faith. Bartimaeus changed his destiny! What does the Lord say? *"I am the vine, ye are the branches. He that abideth in me and I in him, the same bringeth forth much fruit; for without me ye can do nothing"* (John 15:5).

In Roy Hession's book *"We would see Jesus,"* he wrote:

"God draws redeemed individuals into co-operation with Himself in the outworking of His glorious purposes and we become His branches on which His fruit is borne. Without God the branches can do nothing: without branches the vine does not bear fruit. We do not however, produce or initiate the fruit.

That is altogether His work as we faithfully surrender to Him. I have time and again stressed that no believing Christian can accept Jesus Christ as personal Lord and Saviour, lay claim to salvation and new birth, and then go on to live a life based on anything else but faith. That would be absurd! The Word of God declares with clarity and intensity that, 'Therein is the righteousness of God revealed from faith to faith: as it is written, The just shall live by faith' *(Romans 1:17, Habakkuk 2:4; Hebrews 10:38; Galatians 3:11)."*

Conversion is just the beginning of a long pilgrimage of mountain peaks, deep valleys, resting places and even swamps; nevertheless our confidence lies in the fact that from the fall of raindrops to the fall of empires, all is under the mighty providential hand of God. His Word on this point has to be Matthew 10:30-31; *"the very hairs of your head are all numbered. Fear ye not therefore; ye are of more value than many sparrows."*

Test and Testimony

If the just shall live by faith then we can expect to be challenged on every count. Why do we need a challenge? To grow in our faith and confidence in God's Word. How can our confidence in God's Word grow, if we never see it proved in our own life or experience? Without the *TEST* there can certainly be no *TESTIMONY!* Besides if Christ himself was tested – how shall we that are His escape the testing process?

In other words the persecution, the problems and daily negatives are necessary in proving Romans 8:31 where it says, *"If God be for us who can be against us?"* Notice when God has a plan that exceeds human ability to perform, He never speaks or appeals to man's reason.

Then Abraham fell upon his face, and laughed, and said in his heart, Shall a child be born unto him that is a hundred years old? and shall Sarah, that is ninety years old, bear?
(Genesis 17:17)

"Abraham... the heavenly planning service would like to visit you, we think it's time you had a son."

"You've left it a bit late haven't you?! I mean, at seventy five I hadn't really planned on the family."

"Well, God has ordained it that you should have a son."

"But... Sarah, she's old now, and I'm old, and..."

Instead, Abraham moved into faith immediately, allowing God to continue the conversation! He realised that God was serious and anything He spoke, He was able to perform. So Abraham accepted the fact that he was going to have a son, and kept expecting for something to happen every single day!

Twenty years later:

"What's happening Abraham, how are you getting on?"

"Fine, I've now got a whole pile of grandchildren! Since accepting the fact I've got a son, God is planning my grandchildren..."

"I see, so God is planning really big?"

"Yes, He's looking all the way ahead and He's seeing all these things..."

"And you're seeing them too?"

"Yes, faith allows me to look into the future, possess it, bring it into the present and rejoice in it now!"

Abraham the Seer

Abraham called things that were not as though they already were which caused him to walk by faith and not by sight *(see 2 Corinthians 5:7)*. Sure enough Isaac came along but just when Abraham thought that he had made it, with all his joy, future and blessing wrapped up in little Isaac, God went and did something unacceptable! *"Now that you have seemingly made it Abraham, I want you to offer up your success to me."*

Abraham didn't turn around to God in confused anger and say, *"Oh that's a cute idea, why didn't I think of that, offer up my son Isaac...?"* It's important at this point to remember that during those days, certain people were accustomed to offering up their children in similar sacrifices, which God was strongly opposed to and was in the process of abolishing!

Therefore Abraham would also have been very familiar with the facts of his day; how certain pagan rituals required offering up innocent children by burning them on altars... Yet was Abraham's God now expecting the same from him? Abraham must have asked himself, *"Is God planning to bring something to an end while bringing it to a new beginning?"*

God loves to share His secrets but always wants somebody to share them with, who won't then say to Him, *"I don't see how that's gonna help; your thinking is off limits God, that's way too big, it's never gonna work..."* No! God wants us up in the throne-room thinking like HE thinks... Seeing HIS ability, power and provision as it really is... God can *DO* whatever leaves his lips! *(see Matthew 4:4)*

God said enough when he said how Jesus is not coming back for a church that He has got to apologise for. He is going to have a church without spot or blemish... Oh what a job the Holy Spirit has got to do!

God is not anxious, there is no conference up in heaven saying, *"Oh what are we going to do with this lot...!"* *"If we had a better generation than this, we may be able to bring it to an end soon."* No I don't believe that God has got any problems like that, everything is right on schedule, everything is right up to date. God's plan and purpose is being fulfilled all the time and everything that comes against it will only *accelerate* it.

Jesus said, *"If thou canst believe,"* in Mark 9:23, *"ALL things are possible to him that believeth."* The moment you believe what God says all sorts of things start happening. EVERYTHING starts to light up! Consider Stephen in Acts 6:5-8;

And the saying pleased the whole multitude: and they chose Stephen, a man full of faith and of the Holy Ghost, and Philip, and Prochorus, and Nicanor, and Timon, and Parmenas, and Nicolas a proselyte of Antioch:

Whom they set before the apostles: and when they had prayed, they laid their hands on them. And the word of God increased; and the number of the disciples multiplied in Jerusalem greatly; and a great company of the priests were obedient to the faith. And Stephen, full of faith and power, did great wonders and miracles among the people.

The Power Remains in the Anointing

We can see that he was a man full of faith and the Holy Ghost - full of faith and power; faith first *THEN* power. The power *remains* in the anointing, which *abides.* That abiding anointing that does not *LEAVE* only comes upon you when you move out of the realm of the natural into the spiritual realm with faith in God's Word.

Then the power of God comes upon you and enables you to carry out that WORD. God watches over His Word to perform it. We must go on being filled with the Holy Spirit as mentioned in Ephesians 5:18 with the present continuous tense; *"...ever be filled and stimulated with the [Holy] Spirit" (AMP)*.

Therefore we ought to be the best preachers in our own lives! In other words, we *MUST* preach to ourselves! There is no excuse *NOT* to preach faith into our own atmosphere. Take for example when we go to bed at night, we must always end in the positive and not the negative.

Even if we think we are going to have a restless night we must be positive otherwise we'll get just exactly what we have faith for! On the other hand someone else will say, *"I'm saving for a rainy day..."* and sure enough a rainy day comes along! We all receive exactly what we are in faith for.

People continually dig their graves with their own tongues, through the foolish things they say. Laying in bed early one morning someone groaned, *"I think I'm going to have a heart attack...!" (But as Harry Greenwood put it; "Just get out of bed - God is not looking for undercover agents...!")* The *"ONLY"* way out of bed when one feels like that is by *"PRAISE;"* praising God for *His living health in our bodies,* as we continue to live by faith.

Concerning our physical health we must say only what God says. Seven hundred years before Christ Isaiah told us in chapter 53:4-5, *"He bore our infirmities and carried our sicknesses." (Fulfilled in the New Testament in Matthew 8:17 & 1 Peter 2:24.)*

We must come to God with our physical bodies:

"God I'm tired of getting sick and tired! ...I'm tired of, getting sick - getting healed - getting sick - getting healed. Isn't there something more than this...?"

"Yes... you can live in 'My' health."

*"Ooooh... that's new... live in **Your** health."*

"Yes, the same health that I lived in before Calvary, I gave it up at Calvary, that I might have it back in your experience."

"You mean you want to continue in a healthy body...?"

"I wasn't in a sick body before Calvary... I don't want to be in a sick one afterwards..!"

Preaching Victory to Ourselves

Sometimes to get *"into"* something, we must *PREACH* it first! Again, we must not be shy of getting the old mirror out and *PREACHING VICTORY TO OURSELVES*, forcefully preaching health to our own bodies. After all, *HEALTH* is for the Body of Christ, while *HEALING* is for the *"out-sider."* We must *"reach-out"* with healing for them by living in health, which ultimately not only advertises the healing but also the *HEALER!*

I cannot imagine Jesus returning from the mountain one morning like this; *"Urrrrh...#*@"~, cough...#*@"~, cough...#*@"~ splutter... Peter, just tell them there's no ministry to the sick today, I've got influenza. I'll be down tomorrow maybe... or the next day!?"* Nobody would *WANT* Him to minister anyway, in fear they'd catch what He had!

But of course it was the opposite way round, they were sick and touched Jesus and yes they did catch what he had but it wasn't sickness! Jesus never once caught their infectious diseases *(such as leprosy etc.)* no matter who touched him; rather it was they who caught His infectious *(transferable)* HEALING POWER! As a result even the most casual onlooker of that day could have calculated or concluded that... *health is always greater than sickness!*

My son, attend to my words; consent and submit to my sayings. Let them not depart from your sight; keep them in the center of your heart. For they are life to those who find them, healing and health to all their flesh.
(Proverbs 4:20-22 AMP)

Health to all our Flesh

The Word who was with God and was God became flesh and dwelt amongst us *(John 1:14)* we beheld His Glory, the Glory of the only begotten of the Father. He was full of grace and truth. In John 6:63 Jesus said, *"The words that I speak unto you they are spirit and they are life..."* His words were vehicles for the *Spirit* of *Life...*

He sent His Word and healed the sick; that Word is still sent. Everything that came from Him was related to Him, it was as vital as He was. His Word is the same as He is; there is no difference between God and His Word therefore faith in God's Word simply equates to *faith in God.*

The Living Word walked amongst us and as many as touched Him were made perfectly whole. This same Word returned to God after accomplishing all that which was required of Him. We must now walk as He walked, totally free from sickness. Remembering that NOTHING can be lost that was received through a true revelation of the Word.

Right, so once we have preached health to ourselves, do we then imagine that the devil will come along and encourage us by saying; "...*that was a fine message, a real humdinger... that really puts me under your feet doesn't it... I'm really defeated now...!*" If we consider for just a moment, all of us have been attacked straight after receiving a blessing.

The attacks are timely, as Satan only comes to steal, kill and destroy; therefore the enemy of our souls is out to rob our blessing. Yet for our enemy to want to rob something from us – means we must already *HAVE* something worth taking! *(A liar always tries to convince in opposition to truth!)*

As we praise the Lord, instead of just resting on the physical evidence, we come back to the concrete of God's **Word** – which is why we can never lose anything we got by the eternal Word! It's possible to *"have"* a thing and *"lose"* it again, just based on *feelings*, but we can't lose it when our faith is in God's Word.

A good thing for us to discover is that we are *NOT* a body – we live in one. We are a spirit that lives in a shell. Therefore concerning our physical shell - we must learn to live by faith which means living only by what God says concerning it...

However in the event that sickness tries to attach itself to our shell then we can embrace the attitude *"...hold it right there!"* However one must never deny the physical evidence in their body. Although the body might temporarily have it, that does not necessarily mean YOU have it because YOU are a spirit not a body!

God created us in this order, [man from his lowest form to his highest form] body, soul & spirit. Nevertheless now we have been re-created in our spirits we are now in correct order spirit, soul & body. Therefore we should live out from our spirit to our soul, to our body; then to the material realm.

We must know what we have in our spirit before our senses have anything to say! We must know what we have by authority of God's Word first before our physical senses actually communicate to us the physical evidence!

God Heals Because of Faith

In the spiritual realm, we must believe that we've got it before we've got it! Imagine what would happen if everybody believed they were healed before their body knew it? We possess our healing first by our *faith* in God's Word and THEN it comes into our body and manifests *(becomes flesh in our experience)*.

It must be transferred from the spiritual realm – we don't get health from our body - *we get it from the Lord* - so we've got to give it to our bodies by telling our bodies what they've got – before they tell us what they've got! **God heals because of *FAITH*.**

We must quote what the Word of God says *ABOUT OUR SHELL AND TO OUR SHELL!* For example:

I am the Lord that healeth thee... I am and the Lord, I change not... Jesus Christ is the same yesterday, and today, and forever... forget not the Lord and all His benefits: Who forgiveth all thine iniquities; who healed all thy diseases... the Word is life to all those that find it and health to all their flesh... who bore my infirmities and carried my sicknesses... by His strips I was HEALED. (Exodus 15:26, Malachi 3:6 Hebrews 13:8; Psalm 103:2-3)

Then say, **"Thank you Lord, THAT is what I truly HAVE in You."** Only then can we turn over and go to sleep without spending half the night trying to get rid of what we *DON'T* have!! Again, God heals only because of *FAITH. (He has NO favourites!)* Without which we cannot please God; and whatever is not of faith is sin *(Romans 14:23)*. We must not violate Faith. We must live by the *FAITH OF THE SON OF GOD* for our entire man: spirit, soul and body.

I have been crucified with Christ [in Him I have shared His crucifixion]; it is no longer I who live, but Christ (the Messiah) lives in me; and the life I now live in the body I live by faith in (by adherence to and reliance on and complete trust in) the Son of God, Who loved me and gave Himself up for me.

(Galatians 2:20 AMP)

❖

CHAPTER 8

I Need You Holy Spirit

The last verse of 2 Corinthians is a powerful one and the Amplified Version puts it like this: "The grace *(favor and spiritual blessing)* of the Lord Jesus Christ and the love of God and the **presence and fellowship** *(**the communion and sharing together, and participation**)* in the Holy Spirit be with you all. Amen *(so be it)*."

The grace of the Lord Jesus Christ, and the love of God, and the fellowship of the Holy Spirit, [is] with you all! Amen.

(2 Corinthians 13:14 YLT)

Everything in this verse points to a three fold companionship with God. Remembering that one of His names is also "Emmanuel" which means "God with us." This is reflected in the Young's Literal Translation above

85

where it says "...the Holy Spirit *[IS]* with you all!" All three Persons of the Godhead; Father, Son and Holy Spirit, are active in providing this companionship with us. Jesus brings grace and the Father brings love. Both, grace and love are so potent that they can only originate from God *(Ephesians 2:8; John 3:16)*.

His grace allows us "entry" into divine companionship while His love "keeps" this companionship breathing and vibrant. However the Holy Spirit also plays a vital role in ensuring our companionship with the Almighty, and it is HIS "contribution" to this relationship that we focus on in this chapter: **"I Need You Holy Spirit."**

Communion by Intimate Participation

We begin by looking into the Greek meaning for the word "fellowship" used in our opening scripture 2 Corinthians 13:14. This Greek word is "koinonia" that literally means: **communion, communication, contribution, distribution, joint participation, intimacy.** It could be said like this; **"communion by intimate participation!"** However it also involves words like *partnership, (social) intercourse* and *(pecuniary or economic) benefaction - coming from the closely related words* "koinonos" and "koinos" *meaning sharer*, i.e. *associate* :- companion, fellowship, partaker, partner *(see Strong's #G2844 #G2839)*.

So as we can see this Greek word for "fellowship" *(koinonia)* is a complex, rich, and thoroughly fascinating Greek approach to building community and teamwork. It has such a multitude of meanings that no single English word is adequate to express its depth and richness. Therefore however we look at this word, we can derive so much from it in order to help us decipher what is exactly meant or entailed by "fellowship" with the Holy Spirit.

First of all let's break this up slightly for easier grasp - "koinonia" has three superb applications.

Joint Participation

The fellowship of the Holy Spirit is not a one-way street! It is a sharing of wills, feelings, and knowledge. We share what we have or know with Him and He shares what He has and knows with us! Jesus said, "He will tell you whatever He hears *[from the Father; He will give the message that has been given to Him]*, and He will announce and declare to you the things that are to come *[that will happen in the future]*. He will honor and glorify Me because He will take of *(receive, draw upon)* what is Mine and will reveal *(declare, disclose, transmit)* it to you." *(John 16:13b-14 AMP)*.

Just think, He knows the secrets of heaven and is willing to reveal those to whoever will "jointly participate" with Him. The Holy Spirit has direct access to the Father's heart which means whatever the Father speaks; He hears and is able to communicate to us! In other words we can enjoy "inside information" if we will only "dare" to draw closer in fellowship with Him, as we are admonished to do in James 4:8;

Draw nigh to God, and he will draw nigh to you.

The original Greek here for "draw nigh" or "come close" depending on what translation of the Bible you have - literally means: "approach" or "be at hand" for Him. Once we "approach" God like this, or in other words "make ourselves available by being at hand" then God can reciprocate with His presence! He approaches us in return and is always "at hand" for us! What an awesome reality this is. To have God Himself close by and always "at hand!" Can we fathom the beautiful implications of this and the impact that such fellowship can have on our everyday lives?

The only glitch or claws to this "drawing nigh" business of verse 8 of James chapter 4 is that we must "draw nigh" FIRST! Which quite plainly puts the overall "onus" onto us! The quality of the fellowship that we enjoy with God, or the regularity of such - largely rests with us and our willingness to "approach" Him or to be "at hand" for Him.

For sure "any" approach that we make towards God, could be seen only in terms of a "response" to what He has already "initiated" through Christ. For instance according to 1 John 4:19, "We love because he **first** loved us..." *(NIV)* it was God who "initiated" love - not us! In fact we initiated nothing in this context. It came from and started with God. However in terms of **"relationship"** *(the two way street we are discussing here)*, our "willingness" is always a "prerequisite" and must always be evident *(to God and especially to ourselves!)*

As heaven's divine distributor the Holy Spirit equips and prepares us for the future. Through Him we can face any challenge that life throws at us! And within this type of "fellowship" we are able to communicate our intimate and most personal needs; whether desires of the heart or heart concerns and is a type of fellowship that enjoys both "spontaneity and freedom" rather than dictatorial and dull monologue! In this respect we should always freely "welcome" the Holy Spirit into our lives; appreciating, respecting, adoring and fully recognising Him in everything that we do.

Potent Partnership

The type of fellowship that we are discussing here in this particular chapter - represents a most effective and potent partnership! All partnerships exist to enhance growth, productivity and profit. Partners strategise *(manage or management)* together and share in all successes and failures. However when we consider fellowship with the Holy Spirit in this way, then **we must always recognise Him as the "Senior Partner"** *(simply because he brings so much more to the table than we do, the purposes of God!)*

For example consider the infinite resources and knowledge that He possesses; which can only make His strategies and methods perfect and above reproach! In addition regard the fact that no matter how much He outranks everyone, He still leaves room for us to be heard every time!

Strategising on our Behalf

Nevertheless we do well to "allow" Him to strategise on our behalf - as He knows best and the results are always more consistent! We must make ourselves available by always being "at hand" to fellowship with Him, so that He can communicate those strategies with us as He wants to do. We must always "live-ready" to listen to His instruction and be equally willing to receive His specialised help for the "follow-through" of that instruction! The best fact of all is that He not only lends us His expertise but also His "power!"

Remembering that even as partners who share victories - the credit must all be His! He is unable to fail and neither will we if we learn to follow and yield in the manner that we are discussing here. It is elementary then, that in the degree to which we "cooperate" is the degree to which we will experience success in and through our personal lives.

Everything the Holy Spirit does, is to empower us. Therefore we can be certain that "fellowship" with Him, will only benefit our lives. Heaven's intentions can then be realised. It is through deep fellowship like this that History can be changed as a result! NOT sitting in a lotus position meditating and chanting in tongues - that is not "fellowship" - but a religious ritual that some might like to call "fellowship!" But true fellowship with the Holy Spirit is very much "active" and part of our everyday lives.

He talks with us "on the go!" Nothing restricts Him. Not time or space! He is always ready and always willing for us to "plug in" and enjoy our "living-connection" with Him. In fact it should never be broken. We should not spend our Christian lives "travelling-in-and-out-of-His-presence" but learn to LIVE there!

Partnering with Him

In fact the kind of "fellowship" we discuss here is very active and accountable simply because the Holy Spirit specialises in transforming what is "written" instruction from the word of God into practical application in our lives. Therefore it is vital that we learn to partner with Him on every level; being open to His input and advice before making decisions.

I'm not suggesting that we need the Holy Spirit to tell us when to clean our teeth - some things we can work out for ourselves! When to wash and to eat etc; and He gives us enough credit to do that sort of thing on our own! However when it comes to the larger decisions of life - it is a "learnt" discipline - to pass things with Him first. It takes time but we must pursue such a discipline - especially when the end product of living in such a way - has the potential to change other people's lives as a result.

Sensitivity to the Holy Spirit on this level means that He can depend on us to ACT in any given situation - no matter what the circumstances say. This is where we allow the "unction" of the Holy Spirit to dictate our thoughts rather than the conditions of the world around us.

In addition to that is the fact that our obedience has always a good influence on others, even if we cannot directly see the results of it with our own eyes - we can guarantee that if the Holy is in control - He always has others in mind and an agenda that pursues their freedom and liberty! **"Now the Lord is that Spirit: and where the Spirit of the Lord *is*, there *is* liberty"** (*2 Corinthians 3:17*).

It is important to add right now that the Holy Spirit does not just promote the "self-life" that the world does - rather He "demotes" selfishness and "promotes" selflessness! He is not our spiritual maid, who picks up the pieces that we leave behind or our PR who deals with all the "damage-control" in our lives - for all those mistakes we make!

We live in a generation of "self-help" coaches and gurus - who make millions off the back of people who have no identity of their own - we could easily confuse the Holy Spirit with our own "personal-trainer" but I would like to suggest that He is SO MUCH MORE THAN THAT! It is a danger to limit the Holy Spirit to such "earthly" status!

On the other hand, He never "closes-shop" on us and is always available for us. He shares in our failures as much as our successes, so that the challenges of life don't overwhelm us. He moves in us, so that our spiritually-natural instincts are to "overcome" in situations rather than indulge in or enjoy "self-pity" too much!

In fact the world around us is obsessed with "self" - yet in Christ we learn that life is not all about "self" and we soon learn that we don't just exist to avoid or rescue ourselves from ourselves! Instead we learn to "overcome" in ways that help others as a result and with His divine influence upon our lives; normal temptations should be more easily overcome.

This is generally how we know if someone is truly walking with the Spirit of God or not - because if they really know Him *(and are known of Him)*, then the "conviction of Holiness" is always present. This means that they will not feel "well" with themselves, in the presence of sin and will conscientiously work on "adjusting" themselves; in pursuit of maturity and self control. Whereas those who are too comfortable around sin, are probably not walking too closely with the Holy Spirit at all!

For the sake of balance here and in the context of "evangelism" we cannot afford to be overly "delicate" about sin. It is then that we must be open to "embrace" those in the deepest sins - without becoming "one" with their sins in the process. For example Galatians 6:1 *(GW)* says this, "... if a person gets trapped by wrongdoing, those of you who are spiritual should help that person turn away from doing wrong. Do it in a gentle way. At the same time watch yourself so that you also are not tempted."

To continue however, with this application of "potent-partnership" - one of the greatest chapters in the Bible that describes this privileged partnership we have with the Holy Spirit, is Romans 8. The entire chapter is a treasure in fact, but verse 26 just says, "So too the Holy Spirit comes to our aid and bears us up in our weakness..." *(AMP)* What comfort this offers us? With the Holy Spirit "close at hand" like this, everything truly can "work together for good for those who love God" *(vs. 28).*

United Movement

This final application of "koinonia" is taken from another literal translation meaning; **"moving together with..."** We could say "travelling together with...!" As we know, the Holy Spirit excels in the area of "distribution" which can be seen in the context of our prayer lives. For instance He moves or travels with us "as" we pray, by "moving or transporting" our prayer from earth to heaven.

This is indicated in Romans 8:26. As usual the Amplified Version of the Bible puts it more poignantly like this: "So too the *[Holy]* Spirit comes to our aid and bears us up in our weakness; for we do not know what prayer to offer nor how to offer it worthily as we ought, but the Spirit Himself

goes to meet our supplication and pleads in our behalf with unspeakable yearnings and groanings too deep for utterance."

So with all this in mind, when it comes time for the "Grace" *(2 Corinthians 13:14)* to be declared over the people at the end of a meeting - we must all say with much more "conviction" because now we possess a better grasp on its original meaning. Fellowship *(koinonia)* is our greatest life's honour - because it represents a living "companionship, intimacy and working together with" Almighty God.

We must never forget that "KNOWING HIM - IS LOVING HIM" and we must always thank Him for the GRACE, LOVE AND FELLOWSHIP that He has placed in our lives. Hallelujah!

PRAYER

Father I want to walk in divine partnership with Your Spirit. Your provision for my life is complete. He helps me to live for You. Thank You Father for all that You have done for me - especially for giving me Your Holy Spirit. Help me never to grieve Him - as I pursue this life for You. **In Jesus Name.**

CONFESSION

Today I am free because of the Holy Spirit. He takes the freedom that Christ purchased for me at the expense of His own blood and makes that freedom a reality in my daily life. Where He is - there is truly liberty - as Your Word says. I confess right now that the Holy Spirit is at the "helm" of my life. I follow His divine instincts and impulses rather than my own "earthy" ones! I have victory today and EVERYDAY *because I follow His leadings and make myself available to Him. When I make myself "at hand" for Him, He reciprocates, as a result* **I WALK IN FREEDOM.** *Hallelujah!*

❖

Conclusion

It is clear then that our own natural faith is inadequate without the supernatural faith of the Son of God. Without doubt ALL things were provided through Christ, not withstanding His *FAITH,* which he has measured out to us.

For I say, through the grace given unto me, to every man that is among you, not to think of himself more highly than he ought to think; but to think soberly, according as God hath dealt to every man the measure of faith.

(Romans 12:3)

Having then gifts differing according to the grace that is given to us, whether prophecy, let us prophesy according to the proportion of faith.

(Romans 12:6)

For to one is given by the Spirit the word of wisdom; to another the word of knowledge by the same Spirit; To another faith by the same Spirit; to another the gifts of healing by the same Spirit.

(1 Corinthians 12:8-9)

Many of us have been puzzled on meeting non-religious people whose demeanour and posture seem to personify the very fruits of the Spirit, yet without Christ! We marvelled at their genuine sincerity and kindness; while conversely grappling with the very memory of certain Christians we met with much less character and personal discipline!

The nagging question that prevails is; *"How can this be?"* Evidently then, man possesses natural abilities and qualities that legitimately benefit his natural life. As mentioned within this book, natural faith is evidenced in many arenas of life such as the business and sports worlds; which help man in all of his efforts to be successful.

Nevertheless as new creatures in Christ we are commissioned to succeed in both realms. No longer earth bound, we are not limited to one realm. We are still in this world but not of it; therefore we must operate successfully in both the supernatural and natural realms.

Even as Christians we still possess natural faith, but we also possess SUPERNATURAL FAITH, which is the very *FAITH OF THE SON OF GOD*. Only the Faith of the Son of God can truly facilitate our success in the supernatural realm. Mark 16:15-18 is our heavenly mission, which supersedes *ANY* natural mission!

Conclusion

Consequently as the justified, redeemed children of God, it remains our highest and deepest responsibility to live this life not only by our own natural and limited faith but also by the FAITH OF THE SON OF GOD, which has been measured to each of us according to His specific divine purposes *(Romans 8:28)*.

Ultimately we must seek to mirror the very sentiments of Paul the apostle who wrote:

I am crucified with Christ: nevertheless I live; yet not I, but Christ liveth in me: and the life which I now live in the flesh I live by the faith of the Son of God, who loved me, and gave himself for me.

(Galatians 2:20)

Forward or Pass it On!

Note: If this book has blessed you, let it bless others. Share it, and let the message bear fruit in someone else's life. *"What you have heard... entrust to... others"* (2 Timothy 2:2). Why not sow by gifting a copy, or even placing a bundle in the hands of your home group or church? In this way the truth multiplies and glorifies our Heavenly Father.

A massive Thank You

❖
Bibliography

- Capps, Charles. Releasing the Ability of God through Prayer. Copyright © 1978. Published by Harrison House, Inc. Printed in Tulsa, Oklahoma USA.

- Cho, Paul Y. Prayer Key to Revival. Copyright © 1984. Published by Word Books Publisher. Printed in Waco, Texas USA.

- Ekman, Ulf. The Holy Spirit. Copyright © 1995. Published by Word of Life Publications. Printed in Uppsala, Sweden.

- Hagin, Kenneth E. How You Can be Led by The Spirit of God. Copyright © 1978. Published by Faith Library Publications. Printed in Tulsa, Oklahoma USA.

- Hagin, Kenneth E. The Triumphant Church. Copyright © 1995. Published by Faith Library Publications. Printed in Tulsa, Oklahoma USA.

- Hagin, Kenneth E. Why Tongues. Copyright © 1975. Published by Faith Library Publications. Printed in Tulsa, Oklahoma USA.

- Hayford, Jack. Prayer is Invading the Impossible. Copyright © 2002. Published by Bridge-Logos Publishing. Printed in USA.

- Howard-Browne, Rodney M. <u>Flowing in the Holy Spirit</u>. Copyright © 2000. Published by Destiny Image Publishers Inc. Printed in Shippensburg Pennsylvania, USA.

- Isleib, Mary Alice. <u>Effective Fervent Prayer</u>. Copyright © 1992. Published by Touch of Design. Printed in USA.

- Murray, Andrew. <u>With Christ in the School of Prayer</u>. Copyright © 1895. Published by Fleming H. Revell Co. Printed in the USA.

- Prince, Derek. <u>Shaping History through Prayer and Fasting</u>. Copyright © 2002. Published by Whitaker House. Printed in New Kensington, Pennsylvania USA.

- Sumrall, Lester. <u>The Militant Church</u>. Copyright © 1990. Published by Harrison House, Inc. Printed in Tulsa, Oklahoma USA.

- Wallis, Arthur. <u>God's Chosen Fast</u>. Copyright © 1968. Published by CLC Publications. Printed in Washington, Pennsylvania USA.

- Strong, James. S.T.D., L.L.D. 1890. <u>Strong's Exhaustive Concordance; Dictionaries of the Hebrew and Greek Words</u>. e-Sword ® version 7.6.1 Copyright © 2000-2005. All Rights Reserved. Registered trade mark of Rick Meyers. Equipping Ministries Foundation. USA www.e-sword.net.

Bibliography

- Scripture references marked MSG are taken from The Message. Copyright © 1993, 1994, 1995, 1996, 2000, 2001, 2002. Used by permission of NavPress Publishing Group.

- Scripture references marked NKJV are taken from the New King James Version. Copyright © 1982 by Thomas Nelson, 1982 by Thomas Nelson, Inc. Used by permission. All rights reserved.

- Scripture references marked YLT are taken from the Young's Literal Translation of the Bible.

Drs Alan and Jennifer Pateman

are missionaries from the UK,
who at present reside in Tuscany, Italy,
and travel together as an apostolic team. They
are the Founders of Alan Pateman World Missions,
Connecting for Excellence International Fellowship,
LifeStyle International Christian University,
and APMI Publishing/Publications.

*(Please see our website for all profile and
international information, itinerant, conferences
and graduations, etc.)*

www.AlanPatemanWorldMissions.com

❖

To Contact the Author

Please email:

Alan Pateman World Missions

Email: apostledr@alanpatemanworldmissions.com
Web: www.AlanPatemanWorldMissions.com

*Please include your prayer requests
and comments when you write.*

❖

Other Books

Media, Spiritual Gateway

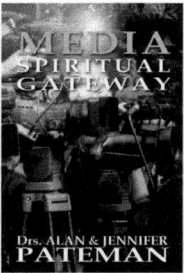

Let's face it; we live in the era of fake news! It's always existed, but never been quite so prominent. Today it's an all-out-war between fact and political fiction.

ISBN: 978-1-909132-54-2, Pages: 192,
Format: Paperback, Published: 2018
Also available in eBook format!

Millennial Myopia, From a Biblical Perspective

The standard for every generation is Jesus. However Millennial Myopia describes the trap of focusing everything on one particular generation or demographic cohort, at the exclusion and expense of all others. The Church cannot afford to make this mistake too.

ISBN: 978-1-909132-67-2, Pages: 216,
Format: Paperback, Published: 2017
Also available in eBook format!

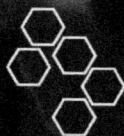

All Books Available

at

APMI PUBLICATIONS

Email: publications@alanpatemanworldmissions.com
*Also Available from Amazon.com
and other retail outlets.*

*If you purchased this book through Amazon.com
or other and enjoyed reading it, or perhaps one of
my other books, I would be grateful if you could
take a couple of minutes to write a Customer
Review, many thanks.*

By Dr. Alan Pateman

BY DR. JENNIFER PATEMAN

AVAILABLE FROM APMI PUBLICATIONS, AMAZON.COM AND OTHER RETAIL OUTLETS